CARNAC
and the
Megalithic Monuments
of the
Morbihan

FRONT COVER: *Massive stones at the western end of the Kermario alignments.*

BACK COVER: *'Sunshine and showers' at the Kermario passage grave.*

RIGHT: *A view towards the Gulf of Morbihan from the top of the chamber capstone of Les Pierres Plates. The upright stone, originally a passage lintel, has several 'cupmarks'.*

PREFACE

The purpose of this book is to provide an introduction and guide to the megalithic remains in the Morbihan region and to answer some of the questions raised by these monuments of Western Europe's first civilization.

A little over 100 years ago, the Carnac museum of prehistory was founded by a Scotsman, James Miln. A well-informed amateur archaeologist, Miln excavated many sites and communicated his enthusiasm for the subject to a local boy, Zacharie Le Rouzic, who subsequently devoted a lifetime to the exploration of the megalithic monuments.

The prehistoric remains found in the dolmens and at the sites in the area by these two archaeologists are preserved in the museum at Carnac. The museum's prehistoric collection is the third most important in Europe and gives a good idea of the material and spiritual life of our ancestors. It contains items that bear witness to human endeavour over 300,000 years, from the old paleolithic era to the beginning of the middle ages, but it is famous above all for the megalith-building period – the neolithic age.

Visitors will be moved by the remains of prehistoric man's daily life: grains of wheat, hazelnuts, carbonized wild pears, fragments of pottery still bearing the imprint of the craftsman's fingers, and stones used for grinding wheat into flour. They can also admire delicately fashioned flint arrowheads, a wide variety of pottery, the beauty and sumptuousness of 'callaïs' ornaments and polished jadeite axes.

Finally, visitors will wonder what were the ideas and impulses behind the building of the megalithic tombs and monuments. This book attempts to reach an explanation by discussing a number of sites in the Carnac area and taking into account the various hypotheses which exist and the many problems which remain.

Anne-Elisabeth Riskine
Curator of the J. Miln–Z. Le Rouzic
Museum of Prehistory, Carnac.

CARNAC
and the Megalithic Monuments of the Morbihan

John Green

Scattered in the countryside around Carnac and Locmariaquer are numerous megalithic remains which, whilst impressive today, cast only shadows of their former glory. It is hoped that this booklet will help create in the reader's imagination the part the monuments played in early man's lifestyle.

Although the map shows the localities of the main monuments, some are difficult to find. However, sites are often marked by large blue *Camping Interdit* signs. If these are not present then asking the local inhabitants will usually bring results and may add to the pleasures gained from exploring the beautiful countryside of southern Brittany.

The megalith-building period (from the Greek *megas* = large, and *lithos* = stone) in north-west Europe began around 5000 BC and lasted in the Morbihan region for about 3,000 years. (It continued in the British Isles for a further 1,000 years, having started correspondingly later there.) Before this period the area was sparsely populated by nomadic groups subsisting on hunting, fishing and gathering berries, roots and shellfish. However, the discovery that settled agriculture was possible with domesticated animals and crop cultivation had been made around 7000 BC in the Near East and knowledge of it spread westwards, both overland and along coastal routes. Production of food on a regular basis and on a relatively large scale enabled the population of what is now known as the Atlantic Province to grow and form communities rather than mere family groups.

With the advent of a more settled population there evolved social hierarchies with divisions of labour to satisfy the needs of both the immediate family and the wider community. Besides the agricultural workers, there were those who made tools, pottery and items of personal or ceremonial adornment, and those who exploited the necessary materials for these products. Communication over a wide area of western Europe is indicated by finds of finished goods and raw materials at considerable distances from their origins.

The development of specialized production and trading is a sign that a true civilization was taking shape. This is further illustrated by the monumental stone structures, which were clearly more than purely functional in design. These works required large-scale organization motivated by some commonly shared beliefs, at least among the leaders or ruling class of the community. At the beginning of the megalithic period such a belief or religion required burying the dead in collective tombs, which continued to be used for several centuries. Remains of both sexes, young and old, have been found, showing that perhaps a whole family or even village may have used a particular tomb. Design of these tombs differed from area to area, changing over time. Eventually the collective tombs were superseded by burial in single graves and megalithic design changed, leading to the creation of free-standing constructions – parallel rows and stone rings – and to the erection of very large single stones or menhirs.

Continued on page 6

FACING PAGE: *Springtime gorse at the Kermario alignments.*

ABOVE: *'Callaïs' beads, flint knives and scrapers and stone axes from the subsidiary burials in the Saint-Michel tumulus. From the Carnac museum.*

OVERLEAF, LEFT: *The interior of Les Pierres Plates, looking from the chamber towards the angle of the passage. Note the 'ribcage' stylization of a 'torso' on the left-hand stone. Different 'torsos' are carved on other stones in the passage (see page 13).*

OVERLEAF, RIGHT: *The chamber of the Crucuno passage grave, which has lost its passage stones and is now used as a hen-house and cycle shed. The farmhouse is in typical Breton style.*

The large standing stones were probably dragged on tree-trunk rollers and erected by means of levers, possibly with the aid of an earth ramp prepared at the edge of the hole so that the stone would topple into it. The capstones of the tombs were also probably dragged up earth ramps, built to the height of the tops of the vertical support stones.

The megalithic culture began in the Stone Age and from around 2500 BC began to be influenced by the innovations of Bronze-Age technology. However, with the advent of peoples using iron tools and weapons, new values were adopted which caused the building of huge stone monuments to cease. Nevertheless, folk memory still lingering today bears witness to their earlier 'power' in pagan ritual, and reverence for the stones was officially forbidden by succeeding civilizations, including the Roman, Carolingian and Norman empires.

The Atlantic Province containing these megalithic monuments extended from Spain to the northernmost part of the British Isles. Associated monuments are found on some Mediterranean islands and in north-central Europe, evidence perhaps of whence the civilization came or at least of a similar cultural heritage. Brittany, near the geographic centre of the province, is rich in megalithic remains and the Morbihan region in particular has examples of the most impressive monuments. These include some of the earliest and grandest tombs, the biggest artificially shaped menhir, and stone alignments without equal anywhere else in the ancient world.

★

LEFT: *Mané Roullarde gallery grave from its northern end. La Trinité-sur-Mer lies down the hill to the left of the photograph.*

FACING PAGE: *Mané Groh, a fine example of a transeptal passage grave with four side chambers. The 6m-long passage faces south-east and the covering mound has not been restored.*

MEGALITHIC TOMBS

Collective burial in stone-built tombs was practised in Brittany by the first settled farmers around 5000 BC, over 1,000 years before the Egyptian pyramids were built. Several designs of tombs, sometimes called dolmens, derived from two main types, seem to have been used in north-west France. The first type are called passage graves and the second gallery graves.

Passage graves

While visitors to the Carnac area usually first encounter the stone alignments, those interested should also seek out some of the passage graves for which this region is archaeologically famous. From what evidence we have, the earliest of these Breton tombs predate any in the other major groups of similar tombs found in southern and western Iberia and central Ireland.

In its simplest form the passage grave is a circular or rectangular chamber approached by a passage or corridor leading from an outside doorway-like entrance. Whilst the passage is normally covered by horizontal lintel stones, two alternative roof-styles were used for the chamber. One method was to use horizontal lintels, and because the chamber was wider than the passage these capstones were often huge, weighing up to 40 tonnes (for example, the tomb on Gavrinis). The alternative method was to form a beehive-shaped roof of corbelled stones, each successively higher course overlapping the one below until the space was completely covered (for example, the tomb on the Ile Longue). Finally, the passage and chamber were covered by a large mound of stones and earth, often held in or supported by a retaining wall of large stones and/or dry stone walling. In most cases this mound has since been destroyed, its stones plundered for building houses, walls and roads, and also in part by natural erosion.

Examples of simple passage grave types are Kercado, Table des Marchands, Gavrinis and Petit Mont. The earliest passage grave remains which have been dated come from Kercado and are from about 4700 BC. Kercado still has its earth mound, 25m in

diameter, surmounted by a standing stone. The mound is surrounded by a stone circle about 8m from the edge of its retaining kerb of stones. (The key to the tomb can be obtained at the château.) Gavrinis, which is 55m in diameter, has an unusually long passage (16m) leading to a chamber 3.5m square. Its superb artistic carvings make it internationally famous. There is a passenger ferry to Gavrinis from Larmor-Baden (except in the winter months).

Gallery graves

These are more widely distributed in France than passage graves, with particularly large examples in the Loire valley. Associated types also occur in northern Germany, Scandinavia and the British Isles. The earliest north-central European gallery graves are of a similar age to the earliest passage graves, but those in the Morbihan region were built around 2500 BC and are thus already somewhat developed from the original form.

The gallery grave consists of a long rectangular chamber inside a long mound, unlike the circular mound covering a passage grave. The long chamber was often subdivided by slabs of stone to form compartments. Perhaps the best examples of gallery graves on the Morbihan coast are Mané Roullarde above La Trinité-sur-Mer and a poorly preserved one near Le Net (Saint-Gildas-de-Rhuys on the Arzon peninsula).

Developments of earlier passage grave styles
Just as church architecture has adopted many styles

★

LEFT: *A passage stone half-way along the Gavrinis tomb. Amid the concentric arcs and sinuous curves are two 'axes'. More realistic axe carvings appear on the other side of the passage.*

FACING PAGE: *The end chamber of Gavrinis. From the chamber, the lines of the passage stones are directed towards the mid-winter sunrise and moonrise at its maximum declination.*

8

in the last 1,000 years, so the styles of collective tombs changed over the 2,500 years in which they were constructed and used. Whilst many tombs display minor deviations in detail, below are summarized the main types to be found in the Morbihan region. Datable pottery finds in the tombs show that these designs were indeed used later than the simple type.

The first type is the wedge-shaped tomb, where there is no distinct separation of passage and chamber, the passage simply widening from the entrance towards the end. Examples are found at Mané Kerioned and Rondossec. Both of these sites have the remains of three passage graves. At Mané Kerioned all three are wedge-shaped, the end pair being parallel and the central one at right angles to them. At Rondossec the central passage is wedge-shaped and one of the others has a side chamber.

Several tombs of wedge shape, with particularly long passages, differ from the simple tombs in that about half-way along the passage they turn through an angle of up to 90 degrees. Le Rocher and Luffang are two examples of the angled passage grave, but perhaps the best known is Les Pierres Plates at the south-western end of the Locmariaquer peninsula. This last example, which has some particularly fine

Continued on page 14

★

FACING PAGE, LEFT: *A representation of a mother goddess (?), almost 2m high, on the backstone of the Mané Lud passage grave. (The 'ghost' is the photographer!)*

FACING PAGE, ABOVE RIGHT: *A hafted axe and other symbols on the underside of the massive capstone of the Table des Marchands chamber.*

FACING PAGE, BELOW RIGHT: *Unusual carvings at the 'underground' passage grave, one of three at Mané Kerioned.*

RIGHT: *The western and central 'above ground' passage graves at Mané Kerioned.*

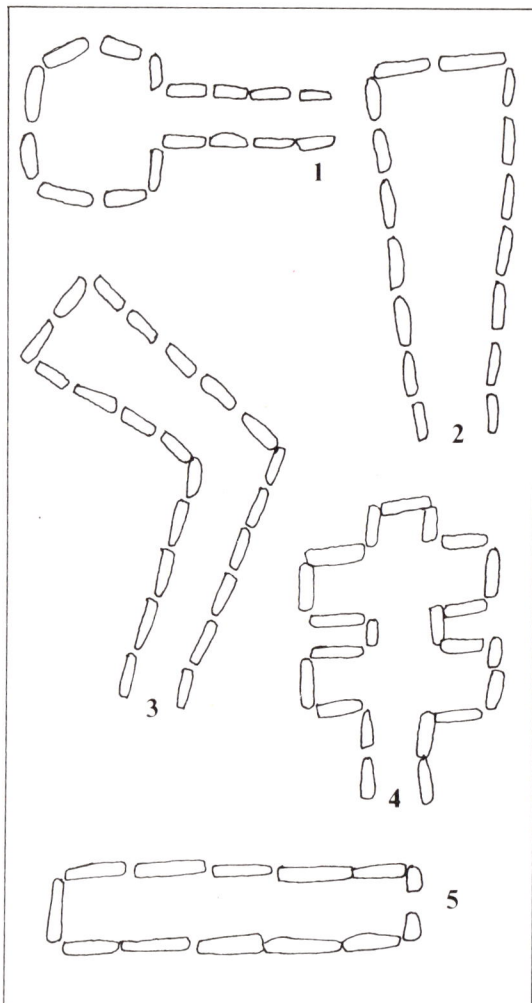

1. Simple passage grave.
2. Wedge-shaped passage grave.
3. Angled passage grave.
4. Transeptal passage grave.
5. Gallery grave.

FACING PAGE: *View into the end of the passage at Mané Bras, north-east of Kerbernes, showing the capstones of three of the four side chambers. The tops of other passage graves on this hillock are also visible.*

ABOVE: *Carvings on the first left-hand passage stone at Les Pierres Plates.*

RIGHT: *The chamber backstone of Table des Marchands. Carvings are also to be found on the other side of this stone.*

13

carved stones, also has a side chamber leading from the angle of the passage.

The third type, the transeptal tomb, is generally a passage grave with one or more side chambers opening off the main passage near its innermost end. Whilst this design is not as common in the Morbihan district as the more simple ones, passage graves with side chambers, often resulting in a cruciform shape, are the more common variety in the major cemeteries in Ireland and the Orkneys. Examples of transeptal tombs are Mané Groh and Keriaval.

Whilst it is likely that all the tombs were covered with earth and stone mounds, some tumuli are impressively large. One example is the Saint-Michel tumulus in Carnac town itself. This mound contained separate burials within several stone settings as well as a more conventional passage grave construction of large stones at its eastern end.

Another very large tumulus once stood to the north of the 'grand menhir brisé' and the remains of the

stone chamber can be seen under the cypress tree across the car park about 150m north-west of the Table des Marchands passage grave.

Whether these very large mounds, sometimes associated with the construction of passage graves, are contemporary with them or with the probably later stone alignments, or date from some period in-between, is still not known for certain.

Tomb ornamentation
Several of the tombs already mentioned exhibit carvings on some of their vertical passage or chamber stones or on the underside of the lintels. The megalithic civilization has left us no evidence of written communication, but the carvings clearly had symbolic meaning as well as being an art form: several motifs recur in many tombs built over a long period of time and are found as far apart as Ireland and the Canary Islands.

The outline of the design was probably scratched on the rock surface and the motif then formed by abrasion with a flint or stone punch hammered with a mallet of wood or deer antler. In many cases the carving consists of one or two motifs cut into only a portion of the stone's surface area. However, the symbolism moves into a clear art form at some tombs, where a simple symbolic design is extended and developed to cover the entire stone in such a way that the contours of the stone itself blend into the overall pattern.

Some of the symbols carved on the stones are clearly representational, such as axe-heads, but the meaning that this symbol had for the ceremonies in the tombs is not clear to us today. An axe-head might signify that those interred in the grave were of sufficient authority to be able to carry arms (swords are still used ceremonially in today's armies); it might show reverence for the society of a more advanced people in another area which used metal tools or weapons: more likely it refers to agricultural needs, the axe being used to fell trees in order to clear the ground for crops and/or for the autumn slaughter of those animals unable to survive the winter. The symbolic importance of the axe is evident not only

from carvings, found also at Stonehenge and in Scottish tombs, but also from beautifully polished stone axes ceremonially deposited in some of the graves.

One motif which is still used today is the circle with projecting rays. Perhaps to prehistoric man it symbolized the sun or moon, or more generally light or warmth or the seasons.

In order to see the carvings the visitor should equip himself with a torch and hold the light near the edge of the stone, so that the design is thrown into maximum relief.

A brief summary of the best carvings must begin with Gavrinis, which exhibits the most artistic examples of axe designs and a bewildering array of clustered arcs, chevrons and serpentine forms on 23 of the 29 upright passage and chamber stones and on the sill-stone in the passage.

Arguably the tomb with the next finest artistic achievement is Table des Marchands. Its backstone is completely covered with four rows of large hook-like designs (corn-sheaves or shepherds' crooks?) contained within a shield-shaped tablet which itself is surrounded by hair-like protuberances (sun-beams?). The gigantic roofstone has on its underside a large carving of a stone axe in its haft.

Continued on page 19

★

LEFT: *Finely polished stone and jadeite axes and a sun/moon (?) disc in the Carnac museum.*

FACING PAGE: *Aerial view of the western end of the alignments at Le Ménec and the Gulf of Morbihan. The church on top of the Saint-Michel tumulus can be seen at the top right-centre of the picture.*

OVERLEAF, LEFT: *View eastwards along the Le Ménec alignments towards the hamlet.*

OVERLEAF, RIGHT: *Western stones of the Kermario alignments reflected in winter rain-water.*

Les Pierres Plates has several different varieties of the human torso motif. Mané Lud exhibits a face-like carving as well as possible boats, which have similarities with Danish Bronze-Age boat carvings. Petit Mont also has a carving which may represent a boat, as well as many others, one of the best preserved of which is a large rayed circle. Kercado has a hafted stone axe on its roofstone, and that of the Kerveresse tomb is covered in 'cupmarks' (small hollows cut in the surface).

Remains found in the tombs

Owing to the corrosive action of the acidic granite soil, organic deposits in the tombs have not survived well. However, enough has remained to give a partial picture of the tomb contents and to enable comparison to be made with other areas where preservation has been better. Organic contents can be dated by means of scientific methods which measure how much of minute amounts of radioactive carbon survive in the remains. All organic objects start with a given proportion of radio-carbon but after death it decays at a given rate. Since the rate of loss over time is known, measuring how much is left indicates how long the object has been there. Another, less accurate, method of dating is to note how the design and style of pottery changes over the centuries. Pottery found with a datable deposit in a grave can be used to assess the age of a tomb where there is similarly styled pottery but no other datable material.

Human interment in the communal tombs was often restricted to the bones alone, bare of flesh. Grave goods deposited by the Stone-Age builders

★

FACING PAGE: *The eastern end of the Le Ménec alignments. The climate of north-west Europe has deteriorated since the alignments were created, giving rise to some boggy areas which previously would have been dry.*

RIGHT: *Autumn mist at Le Ménec.*

and users of the tombs were fairly sparse, limited mostly to pottery and flint items. The later users of the tombs were more generous in their provision for the journey of the dead into the next world. Beautiful polished jadeite, fibrolite and flint axes were placed in the tombs. Many of these axes have never been used and were deliberately broken in half, presumably at the time of burial.

Pendants of semi-precious stone (for example, fibrolite and 'callaïs', or variscite, a bluish-green stone), often taking the form of miniature axes and arrowheads, are particularly common in the Morbihan tombs, as are flint knives and scrapers. Besides remains of human cremation, finds in the Kercado tomb included early simple and un-decorated round-based pots, barbed flint arrow-heads, pendants and stone axes. There was also much later decorated and flat-bottomed pottery associated with the stone alignment period and gold plaques, 'callaïs' beads and pieces of jadeite. Kercado seems to have been used in both the Stone and Bronze Ages (and, incidentally, also re-used in the Iron Age, perhaps still retaining its religious function for the post-megalithic people).

The remains of bodies found in the apparently most important grave in the Saint-Michel tumulus had been cremated. High-quality grave goods, including many large polished axes of local semi-precious stone, were found with the cremated bones but the other burials had fewer and lesser-quality possessions with them. Also buried in this tumulus

★

LEFT: *The carved Manio menhir marks a tomb subsequently overrun by the eastern end of the Kermario alignments.*

FACING PAGE: *View south-west along the Kermario alignments from the Kermaux windmill. The large stones at the left mark one end of a part-row not parallel with the main alignments.*

ABOVE: *The serpentine carvings below ground level on the Manio menhir.*

FACING PAGE: *A huge, rotund stone at the western end of the Kermario alignments. Round stones may have had female and tall stones male symbolism.*

were the remains of an ox. The Mané Lud tumulus covered a stone setting with a horse's skull placed on the top of each stone.

MEGALITHS

The first megalithic monuments greeting the visitor to the Carnac area are usually its unrivalled stone alignments. Over 2,500 stones, some more than 4m tall, are placed in an area up to 100m wide and about 4km long, with small gaps between four main sections. There are also near-circular settings and single large standing stones. Remains which have been found of objects accidentally or deliberately placed in the material used to refill the holes prepared for the stones suggest erection dates after the building of the passage graves had ceased. The stone-row builders buried their important dead in individual smaller graves, which remain today as low earthen humps (tumuli), as well as in the earlier tombs. Bronze-Age graves often contained a pot, perhaps originally containing beer or mead – giving the society the name of Beaker people – as well as personal possessions. Bronze axes are found for the first time in these graves, dating from 2500 to 1500 BC.

Two major concentrations of alignments are to be found in the Morbihan area: the best known are those 1km north of Carnac and the others are near Erdeven. Early this century Zacharie Le Rouzic carried out an extensive reconstruction of these alignments. Each stone he re-erected was marked on its side by a red plug of cement about the size of a postage stamp.

The Carnac alignments – Le Ménec

The western end of the Carnac alignments is situated on the edge of Le Ménec hamlet. From here almost 1,100 stones in the remains of 12 rows stretch north-eastwards for over 1km. The northernmost ten of these rows are reasonably complete at the western end, whereas the eleventh and twelfth are very incomplete, because stones were taken for constructing the road and nearby hamlet. The rows are not equidistant from one another but become progressively closer together towards the outer rows. They seem parallel but in fact they tend to converge eastwards so that the design is like a gigantic narrow fan. Half-way along their length the rows all bend northwards through about 6.5 degrees. The majority of the stones are about 1m high but towards the eastern end the average height increases to 1.5m and, more impressively, those near the hamlet average near 3m. Statistical analyses based on accurate surveying recently carried out by Professor Alexander Thom suggest that originally the stones were equispaced along the rows approximately 2m apart. If indeed this were the case, with 12 complete rows there would have been about 7,000 stones in this section of the Carnac alignments.

Remains of near-circular features marked by close-set stones are found at either end of this Le Ménec sector. These are discussed later.

Kermario

The massive stones of the Kermario rows begin 250m from the eastern end of the Le Ménec alignments. These rows cover a similar area, over 1km long by 100m wide, with over 1,000 remaining stones. Again the western stones are much larger than those in other parts of the alignment. Professor Thom's survey reveals the Kermario design to be more complex than that of the Le Ménec rows. There seem to be seven main equispaced rows, which show three changes of direction. The westernmost 100m of these stones are on parallel curves rather than in straight rows. South of these seven rows, near the road, are three further straight rows or part-rows. The southernmost of these rows points towards the remains of a fine passage grave which was built long before the rows were constructed.

The eastern end of the Kermario rows is today separated from the main group by the Ravin de Kerloquet which has been artificially flooded. There are probably submerged stones. A tall stone, called Manio, near the eastern end of the alignment, has parallel sinuous carvings near its base below ground level. This stone is thought to mark the site of an earlier Stone-Age tomb which at a later date was

surmounted by the stone alignments. As at Le Ménec, the rows get gradually closer together towards the east; at Manio the distance between them is less than half that near the curved western end.

Kerlescan

Four hundred metres east of the end of the Kermario sector there is a barrel-shaped arrangement of 39 stones. The eastern side of this runs almost due north-south and consists of a row of 18 large stones, contiguous in places. Over 300 stones form 12 or 13 lines extending east from this row for about 300m, again in a fan shape.

Petit Ménec

The final sector of the Carnac alignments starts about 250m further east, beyond the farm and across the road. Remains of some 200 stones hide amongst the undergrowth and light woodland. The design is not clear, but the main feature has about half the stones in a wide curve consisting of two or three rows over 300m in length. The remaining stones form a fan shape of six or seven rows about half-way along and adjacent to the south-east portion of the curve. It is possible that Kerlescan and Petit Ménec once formed part of a single design.

The Erdeven alignments – Kerzerho

The principal section of the Kerzerho alignment, much restored, begins about 1km to the south-east of the village and formerly continued south-eastwards for over 2km. The eastern end is also restored. It probably consisted of over 1,100 stones in ten rows. Other short rows are found in the vicinity: one of these, north of the west end of the main section, has several very large stones running perpendicular to the main direction. These part-rows seem unrestored and thus their relationship to the main rows is unclear.

Less impressive alignments in the Carnac area can be found at Sainte-Barbe and at Saint-Pierre on the Quiberon peninsula.

Stone circles

Whilst stone circles (sometimes locally called 'cromlechs') are relatively common in the British Isles and stone rows rare, the opposite is true in Brittany. Five of the Breton cromlechs are clearly associated with the stone rows and it is thought that another once existed at the west end of the Kermario rows. At each end of the Le Ménec rows is an oval cromlech. The western one partly surrounds the hamlet and its stones are contiguous in places. One hundred metres north-west of the Kerlescan rows, and immediately north of the barrel cromlech, is the largest circle, over 35 stones of which can be found, with difficulty, in the undergrowth of the woodlands. When complete, this cromlech shaped like a flattened circle must have been over 200m in diameter.

Professor Thom's survey of the stone rows was extended to cover these four cromlechs. Whilst none is truly circular, the stones are not randomly placed but appear to lie in shapes which are also found in the British Isles and which were apparently chosen to conform to some long-forgotten ceremonial need. Thom suggests that this involved the use of whole-number units of length and a knowledge of those right-angled triangles whose sides' lengths are whole numbers. (The first recorded knowledge of such triangles was given by Pythagoras many centuries later.) Two oval-shaped circles tangential to one

★

ABOVE: *The entrance to the passage grave at the south-western end of the Kermario alignments.*

FACING PAGE: *Autumn sunlight dappling the stones of Petit Ménec.*

another occur on the Ile d'Er-lannic, an island less than 100m across in the Gulf of Morbihan. At high tide all of one circle and half of the other are submerged and consequently we cannot today be sure of the complete design of these circles or of any other features, traces of which may have been washed away by tidal races. Sea level has risen in this area since Roman times and before then the Ile d'Er-lannic and other islands in the gulf, on some of which there are tombs, would have been low hills standing out from a plain.

A cromlech is associated with the stone rows at Saint-Pierre and another, consisting of well-spaced stones, surrounds the Kercado tomb. It is not known if this was built at the same time or after the tomb, but a similar design exists at Newgrange in Ireland and there it is thought that circle and tomb were contemporary, albeit built about 1,000 years after Kercado.

Two other stone settings deserve mention. East of Crucuno near Erdeven there is a rectangular construction whose sides accurately align north-south and east-west. However, the site has been restored and it is thus not certain that this was the original intention. The other setting is a quadrilateral of low contiguous stones in the woods 200m north of the east end of the Kermario alignment and near the large menhir known as 'le géant'. Le Rouzic suggested that this design originally enclosed a mound of earth and/or stones which have since disappeared.

★

FACING PAGE: *The western contiguous stones of the 'barrel-shaped' Kerlescan cromlech.*

RIGHT: *A menhir 70m north of the centre of the western arc of the 'barrel' cromlech, marking the western end of a tumulus. This is one of the menhirs Thom suggests was intervisible with 'le géant', forming a key solar direction. The other large cromlech is 80m due north of this stone.*

Standing stones

While single standing stones (or menhirs) are found over a wide area, many of them are associated with the megalithic tombs. One still remains on the summit of the Kercado passage grave and others are found in their immediate vicinity, for instance at Table des Marchands and Le Moustoir. Unlike the tombs, carvings on the menhirs are rare. In the Morbihan region there is an axe carving on the menhir at Kermarquer en Moustoirac, five 'serpents' carved at the base of the Manio menhir in the Kermario alignments, one carving on the menhir at Crucuny and on some of the menhirs of the Er-lannic circles.

The tallest standing stone (6m) to be seen in the Morbihan region is 'le géant', near the quadrilateral stone setting already mentioned. Today it stands in woodland but this was probably not the case when it was erected. In a treeless countryside other menhirs would have been visible from it, including a fine menhir between the Kerlescan cromlechs, Manio and menhirs at both ends of the Le Ménec alignments.

The intervisibility of pairs of menhirs may have been the reason for their positioning. Two stones are sufficient to determine a direction and the further apart they are, the more accurately this direction is determined. Professor Thom has studied the relative location of many menhirs in the surrounding countryside and has suggested that the directions determined by such intervisible menhirs indicate some of the positions on the horizon of moon and sun rising and setting at significant points of the calendar. This explanation of the siting of menhirs cannot be proved so long after the event; but this suggestion coincides with similar associations of some mega-lithic monuments with the calendar in the British Isles.

Most of the megaliths in the alignments are stones in their natural state, dragged to their current position and then erected. However, some of the single menhirs have been artificially shaped, possibly using fire and water (by heating the stone along the line to be fractured and then throwing on cold water

and pounding the desired break point). The largest artificially shaped stone in Europe is to be found, now broken into four pieces, near the Table des Marchands. This menhir, called Er Grah or 'le grand menhir brisé', was once about 21m long and weighed over 300 tonnes. It is thought to have been dragged from the western side of the Quiberon peninsula from an outcrop of rock now submerged. There is no reliable record confirming that it once stood upright; but the position of the fallen pieces does suggest that it did once stand intact and then tumble, possibly as a result of an earthquake or lightning. When upright, the 'grand menhir' would have been visible from places as far away as the Arzon and Quiberon peninsulas and from Le Moustoir, north of the Kermario alignments. Findings of Bronze-Age remains at key sites at these places suggest they were contemporary with the menhir. When viewed from these places the menhir would have determined important lunar directions, as would 'le géant' and its sightlines with possibly associated menhirs.

WHY WERE THE MONUMENTS ERECTED?

The archaeological record only identifies the tangible remains of the civilization that built the megalithic monuments. Without records that can be interpreted with certainty, we will never fully understand this civilization's culture. The following suggestions are

★

LEFT: 'Le géant', due north of Manio, is the tallest stone now standing in the Morbihan area and, significantly for a 'foresight' marking a direction, is on the highest hill in the neighbourhood.

FACING PAGE: The 'quadrilateral' is 50m north-west of 'le géant'. The path to these sites starts between the eastern end of Kermario and the Kerlescan 'barrel-shaped' cromlech, to the west of the equestrian stables. Walking north, one then takes the path to the left signposted 'Quadrilateral'.

28

thus conjectures which fit some of the archaeological evidence.

It is plausible that any civilization which was at the mercy of the climate to the extent that the first farmers were, would have adopted a natural religion in the hope of ensuring sunshine and showers in the desired proportions. Seasonal change would have had to be recorded in order to know the correct time for seed-sowing. The daily, monthly and annual cycles of sun and moon were an obvious choice as natural timekeepers.

The sun's death each evening and its successful rebirth at sunrise may have symbolized to Stone-Age man his natural desire for reincarnation, as indicated by the grave goods left for the journey of the dead into the next world. This would mark the tomb as a sacred place where the living worshipped the illustrious dead and hoped in turn for their blessing.

The seasonal cycle parallels the stages of human existence – spring, summer, autumn and winter corresponding to birth, adulthood, death and the wait for rebirth. It is likely that there were seasonal ceremonies at the tomb to mark the key times of harvest, mid-winter, etc. It is significant that one of the most magnificent megalithic passage graves of the Atlantic Province, Newgrange, was specially constructed (about 3300 BC) so that a shaft of sunlight could penetrate its end chamber only around the shortest day of the year.

Another likely aspect of a natural religion would be fertility rites linked with the spring birth of the animals and sprouting corn. Stone-Age tombs have contained crude mother-goddess figurines, some with exaggerated breasts and buttocks. The human torso carvings at several Morbihan tombs are thought to represent the earth-mother goddess. The shape of the tomb and often associated standing stones may represent reproductive organs symbolizing life coming from the tomb.

Over the centuries changes in religious beliefs and associated ritual were reflected by changes in the monumental architecture. Possibly the change from collective tombs to single burial, with improved-quality grave goods, marked a shift towards

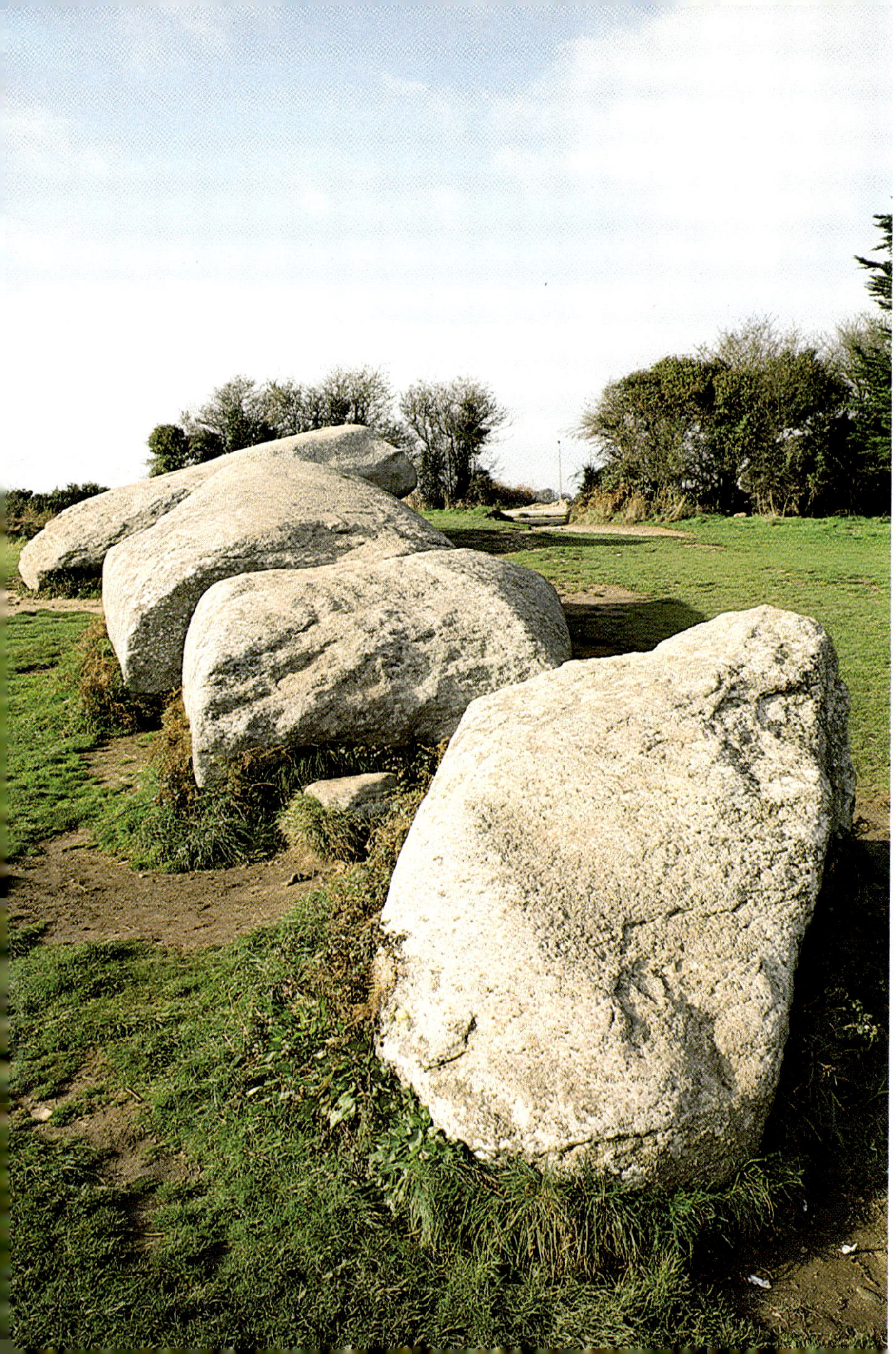

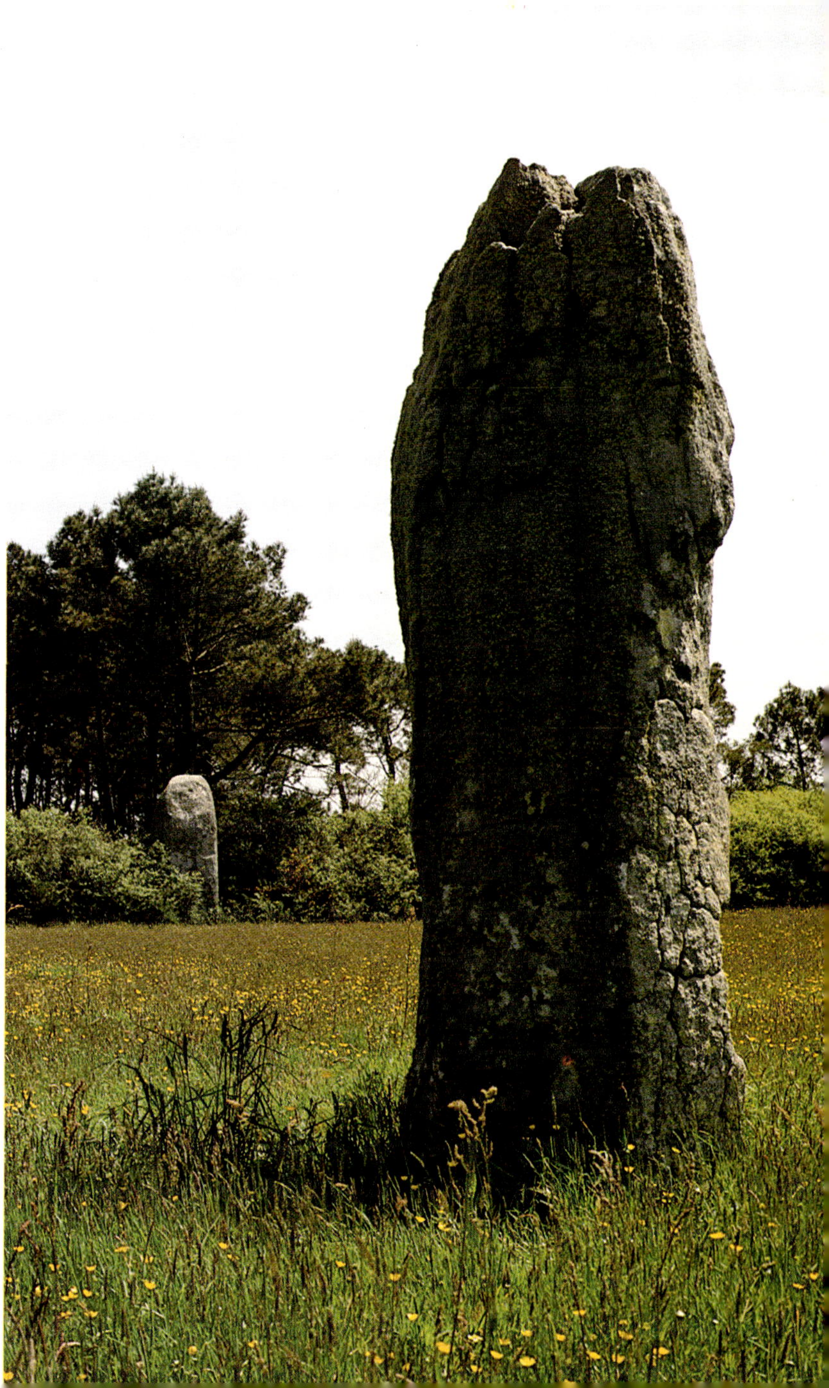

reverence for the successful individual rather than for society as a whole. The similarity of passage leading to chamber and stone alignment leading to stone circle is worth noting. Perhaps the leadership/priesthood felt more secure, so that instead of a few priests involved alone in the tomb/temple, the whole population could take part in proceedings carried out at an open-air site.

If the religion did involve the sun and moon as 'timekeeper' gods, then their worship would have involved noting their movements in the sky. The positioning of standing stones in Brittany and Britain is consistent with such a hypothesis. Besides having the well-known major sightlines approximating to sunrise on the longest day and sunset on the shortest, Stonehenge, which was redesigned several times between 2300 and 1500 BC, may also mark key lunar positions. The power of the priesthood would be enhanced by any technology it could incorporate into its knowledge of the movement of the heavenly bodies. It has been suggested that some megalithic designs, including the fan shape of the alignments, were used to determine key dates more accurately by extrapolating from two or more sightings, and even to predict eclipses.

Whilst the above is only conjecture, recorded folklore and myth have many links with these hypotheses. The Christian religion followed only

★

FACING PAGE, LEFT: *The fallen 'grand menhir brisé' which, when upright, could have marked key lunar directions with other sites as far as 15 km away on the Quiberon and Arzon peninsulas.*

FACING PAGE, RIGHT: *The pair of menhirs at Kerderff.*

RIGHT: *The tumulus and nearby menhir at Le Moustoir. The tumuli of Le Moustoir, Saint-Michel, Mané-er-Hroeck and Tumiac are examples of huge tombs known as Carnac-type mounds, up to 100m long and 10m high.*

1,000 years or so after the European Bronze Age and absorbed many of its features, including renaming the holy days and arranging the Christian calendar to coincide with them. The sites of churches were often associated with megalithic remains: for instance, the position of the church of Saint-Michel on the Carnac tumulus shows a continuing reverence for, and perhaps desire for domination of, the site.

In more modern times the Breton alignments were still believed to have fertility powers; and folklore suggests that many megaliths in north-west Europe were meant to represent people turned to stone, often at times of weddings (fertility). In Brittany, until the last century, the ossuary on the side of a church was respected together with the community enclosure where the living could look after the remains of the dead and in turn the spirits would look after the living.

These brief explanations and hypotheses give no more than the bare outline of what the Stone and Bronze-Age psyche may have been; but they do serve to show that the people of the megalithic society, who were physically similar to ourselves, also had their own needs, hopes and fears, not substantially different from ours today.

LEFT: *Winter sunset at Kermario.*

★

ACKNOWLEDGEMENTS

All the photographs in this book are © John Green, except that on p.15, from the Musée de Bretagne, Rennes.

The map on the inside front cover is by the Robert Clarke Studio Ltd, from IGN map 1:50 000, sheet 0821, © IGN, Paris 1981, authorization no. 99-0072. IGN agents in the UK are McCarta Ltd.

The author and publishers would like to thank Professor R. J. C. Atkinson and Madame A. E. Riskine for their kind and generous help in the preparation of this book.

ISBN 0 85372 354 0